LINCOLN PEIRCE'S

BiG NATE

ACTIVITY BOOK

THIS BOOK BELONGS TO

_____

Hey there! If this book has fallen into your hands, you're probably one of two things:

1. Awesome
2. On your way to becoming awesome

If you're the first, <u>welcome!</u> You're totally in good company. If you're the second, you're in the right place. I'm Nate Wright. I've been perfecting my approach to awesome for a long time and now, at *great personal cost to myself,* I've decided to take you under my awesome wing. The journey ahead will be tough, but remember . . . if it were easy, <u>everyone</u> would be awesome!

If you really want to be awesome, the first step is to surround yourself with awesome people. Good friends can act as accomplices, confidantes, and in an emergency— scapegoats. Who are your best friends? Put a picture of your friends here! If you don't have one, draw one for now and take a picture the next time you guys all hang out!

STICK YOUR
PHOTO HERE!

4

If you're going to be under my tutelage, you should tell me a little about yourself! Of course, you know all about me and I'll teach you all about P.S. 38 soon, but let's get to know each other! What's your . . .

Name: _____

Favorite Color: _____

Favorite TV Show*: _____

Favorite Movie: _____

Favorite Food: _____

Favorite Animal: _____

Favorite Book Series*: _____

* besides *Big Nate*, of course.

Remember when I said I'd teach you all about P.S. 38 some day? C'mon, it was literally one page ago, keep up! Well, today is that day! Welcome to P.S. 38, a school that has seen better days. Some people consider it a prison, but I prefer to think of it as a playground! And not just because of its actual playground . . .

What's your school like? _____

_____

Who is your favorite teacher? _____

_____

What is your favorite subject? _____

What's your favorite room in your school?

_____

What do you eat for lunch? _____

_____

What's something super
unique about your school?

_____

_____

Your first stop on **Big Nate's School Tour** is my locker!
A one-stop shop for supplies, conversation, and culture!

Now, to the untrained eye, my locker might be a mess, but
there is a method to my madness! Help me find a few things
in here before I'm late for class.

Speaking of culture, is that my yogurt? Can you spot any
cheezy snacks? They're my favorite!

It's not always easy, but sometimes it's worth it to pay attention in class. Just the other day in Mr. Galvin's class, we learned about *Rube Goldberg machines*. Rube Goldberg machines accomplish a simple task in the most over-complicated and inefficient way possible, not unlike the DMV or the Rackleff Public School System.

Using the items provided below and a little ingenuity, create your own Rube Goldberg machine.

BOOT

BUCKET

BROOM

DOMINOS

ROPE

MR. GALVIN
P.S. 38's Science Teacher
for over four decades

DRAW YOUR RUBE GOLDBERG MACHINE HERE!

9

Part of being awesome is keeping the fans happy. Now, what do my fans like most? **Pranks!** The ol' sign switcharoo has been around forever. Take the letters on the sign below and rearrange them to say something funny!

WELCOME
BACK TO SCHOOL,
CLASS—OF P.S. 38—
DON'T FORGET
TO SHARPEN
YOUR PENCILS!

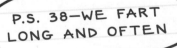

P.S. 38—WE FART
LONG AND OFTEN

10

Ahhh, **P.S. 38.** The best part about this place is that the hallowed halls of learning are shaping the minds of the next generation (or whatever). The second-best thing is that lots of twisting hallways means lots of places to hide when you're on the run.

Speaking of which, you haven't seen Mrs. Godfrey anywhere, have you? Asking for a friend.

Detention. Unfortunately, it is a natural and inevitable part of being awesome. The more awesome you are, the more the un-awesomeness of the world will try to hold you back. Until you've earned your own detention slips, here are a few blank ones I swiped from Mrs. Godfrey. Make them say whatever you like, and maybe even hand them out to your friends!

DETENTION

NAME:_____ DATE:_____

LENGTH OF TIME:_____

REASON FOR DETENTION:
_____
_____
_____
_____

DETENTION

NAME: _____ DATE: _____

LENGTH OF TIME: _____

REASON FOR DETENTION: _____
_____
_____
_____
_____

DETENTION

NAME: _____ DATE: _____

LENGTH OF TIME: _____

REASON FOR DETENTION: _____
_____
_____
_____
_____

13

There are important rules to the fine art of pranking. For one: Always remember, if you dish it out, you gotta be able to take it! Find these pranking mainstays in the word search below.

```
M S R T J A C A B B A G E L I
G E P X S L K T U Q R I I A G
F K U I M U E I P Y U X D M U
P A M G D R J A C K L Y N P H
F H K J R E H B A H H V I A B
H K E A U L R Y L Z F Q Z Q C
W T N M U U E J U Y E L O O C
F C I F W B Y E N R T X R M Z
E M Z A F W Y H V R S X R D U
I F D V F N G K Y F I G M B D
E J P K E B K I W I M J D C L
Q P O R G S Z X Y M R H Q F E
U M U W I Q S G U J A W P P Z
D A G Q R K V J C V K W V J N
L Q X N K X D W N R K O C E C
```

SNAP GUM   FAKE ROACH   JOY BUZZER

WHOOPIE CUSHION   EXPLODING TOILET

CHECK THE ANSWER KEY ON PAGE 116. BUT NO CHEATING!

NATE'S TOP PRANKS

Part of being awesome is responding to your adoring fan base. I've pulled just about every prank there is and let me tell you, some have gone over better than others!

Learn from my mistakes and use this space to plan your very own epic pranks!

~~Gum blocking the water fountain~~

Bugs!

Toothpaste cookies

Flour in the hair dryer

~~Mayonnaise Donut~~ (DO NOT MIX UP DONUTS!)

~~Loose Spider~~ (Spider has still not been recovered)

Caramel Onion

Clock Swap

> I LIKE THE WAY YOU THINK!

_____

_____

_____

_____

_____

* Nate Wright is not responsible for any consequences resulting from these pranks!

15

Sometimes when you're telling a story, words just aren't enough! Use the comic panels throughout this book to draw your own stories. Is a monster attacking the city? Have aliens invaded the cafeteria? Not even the lines of the boxes can stop you; the only limit is your imagination!

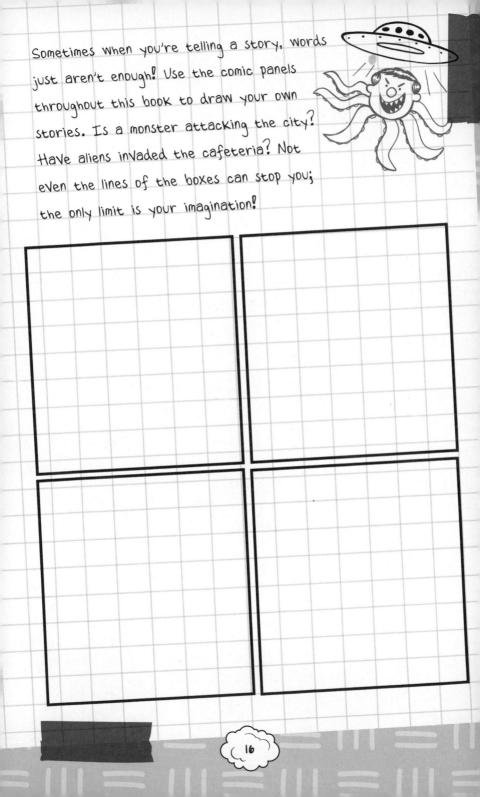

It's that time of year! Time for P.S. 38's school play! Of course, my friend Dee Dee is going way over the top, as usual. She's calling herself Samantha Jade, Private Eye and says she won't stop until she solves some mysteries. Help ~~Dee Dee~~ Samantha Jade find five things that don't belong in the scene below.

Here's a hot tip: It's not cool to say you're awesome. It's cool to _be_ awesome and let others connect the dots. Let's practice by . . . well, connecting the dots.

Once you're done, color in Spitsy!

It takes a keen eye to be the coolest kid at school. You have to watch out for what your fans want and keep an eye on the hot new trends! To the chronically un-awesome, that can seem like a chore, but I'm sure you're up to the task! Spot four differences in these pictures of my friend, Chad!

My dad is a good guy. Heck, maybe even a <u>great</u> guy! That doesn't mean he's without his, uhh . . . quirks, like being terrified of public bathrooms. Help Martin find a **safe bathroom** by solving the maze below!

START

The only way to survive middle school is to have friends by your side.

Who are your best friends? _____

_____

_____

Where did you meet them? _____

_____

_____

How long have you been friends? _____

_____

_____

What's your best memory together? _____

_____

_____

_____

_____

DOODLE PAGE

An astronaut exploring the depths of space.
A cowboy who wrangles dinosaurs. A superhero
who gets his powers from cheese! Nothing is more
awesome than letting your imagination run wild.
Check in with the doodle pages placed throughout
this guide to scribble, scrawl, and jot down
whatever is on your mind.

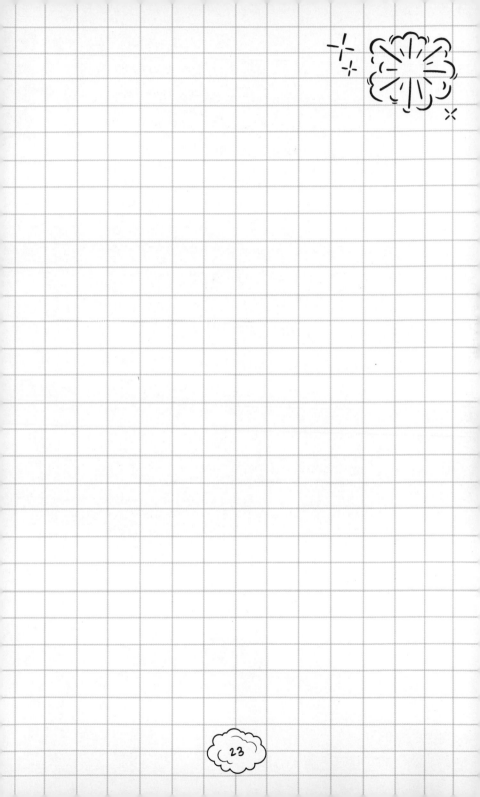

Feeling super? Meet Ultra-Nate, my superhero alter identity! He's super strong, he's super fast, he can fly . . . and best of all? He doesn't have homework tonight! In the space below, draw your own superhero alter-ego, and then give them a fancy suit!

It seems like you're starting to get the hang of this, so I'm going to let you in on something. My friends and I have been using this secret code for years now. Decipher the message below, you'll find more just like it throughout the book.

HEY, GANG! DECODE MY SECRET MESSAGE!

Notebooks aren't just for doodles and making comics, they're also a great place to journal or talk about how you feel. Use this page to write down how you're feeling today and what's on your mind.

Part of being awesome is learning to see the awesome in the everyday. I call it **Nate-O-Vision.*** Take the cafeteria for example. While it may look like nothing but tables and chairs, it would also make a perfect gerbil racetrack! Use your imagination to add whatever you like to this scene.

*patent pending, please don't steal.

Fear the Mollusk is the greatest band in the world! Color in our band logo to help us have a rocking show, then write your favorite bands or musical artists in the spaces below!

1. FEAR THE MOLLUSK

2. _____

3. _____

4. _____

Starting a band isn't hard! All you need is a melody and some rocking lyrics. Use the lines on this page to brainstorm your big hit. For bonus points,* turn it into an actual song!

*bonus points can not be redeemed or exchanged for cash or Cheez Doodles, just a general sense of awesomeness.

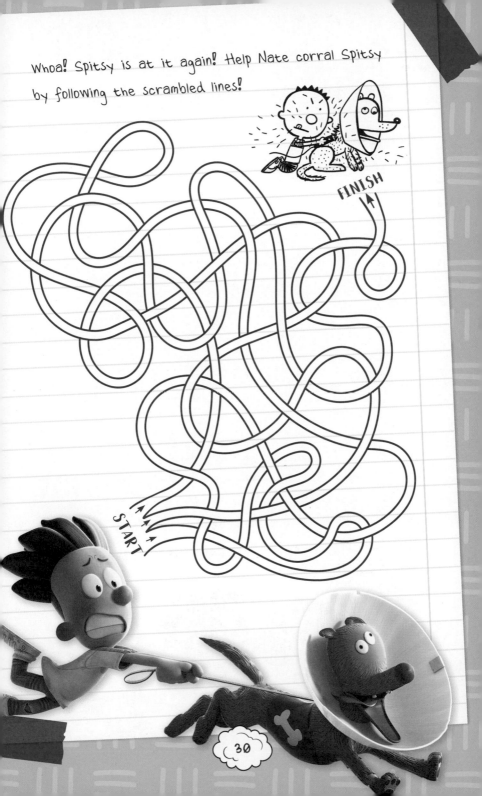

Whoa! Spitsy is at it again! Help Nate corral Spitsy by following the scrambled lines!

FINISH

START

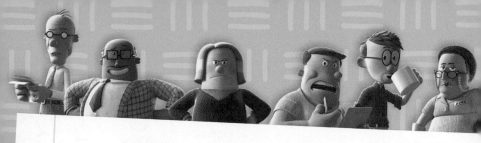

Nate has an idea for the prank of a lifetime, but first he has to make sure there are no teachers around! Help Nate pull off his greatest bit by accounting for all of the teachers in the word search below!

```
H Q B R Y W U Q G L
Y F Z O R A D J O A
T V D A G B Z O D G
R G F R A W H H F A
S O D P L P E N R Z
U I S K V K E J E E
F D I A I Y Z B Y C
E U L R N E K P V W
K B V K U M E H E F
B E N I C H O L S S
```

GODFREY   NICHOLS   GALVIN   ROSA
ZORA   JOHN   LAGAZE

31

We all love going home at the end of the school day, but no one leaves until everything is tidied up! Circle six things in the picture below that seem out of place.

The only thing that scares me is not being remembered as legendary! Well, that and Mrs. Godfrey. Write about a time that you were scared! How did you get past your fear?

Is something off about Dee Dee?

Find and circle **six differences** between these two pictures.

Sometimes being awesome requires outside-of-the-box thinking. Looking at one thing and seeing what it could be instead! With that in mind, how many words can you make out of **NATE WRIGHT**?

NATE WRIGHT

WART

TWANG

Social studies getting you down? Nothing to do in the back of your math class? Maybe a quick comic will relieve your boredom? Make a comic about getting caught doing a prank!

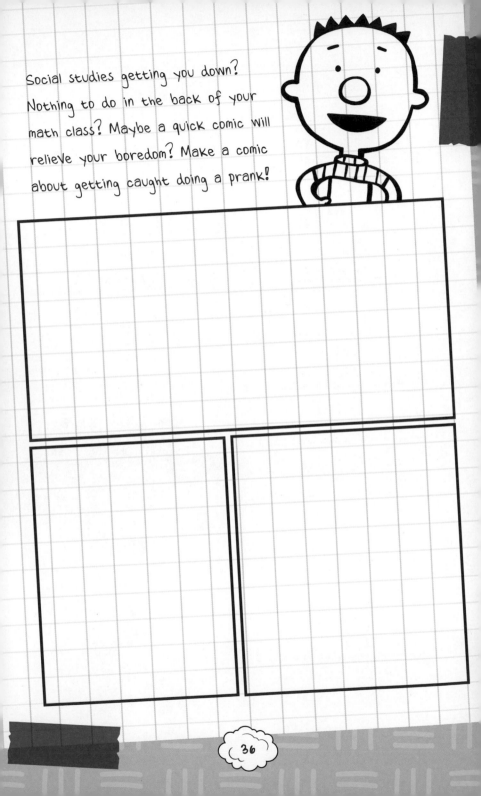

Whenever we have a substitute teacher, Mrs. Godfrey makes sure to leave them a class list. Help today's sub find my classmates' names!

```
E F Q X D H T R O X J P I F G
L Z R U S Q E R X N N F H M I
E P D A G A D R Q E A J M E S
K Y X D N O D V J K F X B B Q
Y X A T N C Y X S Q Y N N E J
T H T T X I I V G K Z U U O N
C J X W O H B S I O D O N B Q
X P K N K S C S E G I N A D Y
S I E R A B S W T J I F B O V
M T P Y G K W E M X D R C N E
B R K B B F C E L R W X A Z R
X X I O N U X D H M O T X D A
I R V B O F K E T U E N G N N
D Y Y G U E T E A G G O O T D
A R T U R N B D J S A A B R Y
```

ARTUR   CHAD   DEEDEE   FRANCIS   GINA
JENNY   KIM   NATE   RANDY   TEDDY

DOODLE PAGE

It's time to flex those doodling muscles of yours! And just like I always tell myself, those are the only muscles you need. Use these two pages to draw anything that comes to mind. Lava sharks, aliens eating hamburgers . . . The only limit is your imagination and the space on the page!

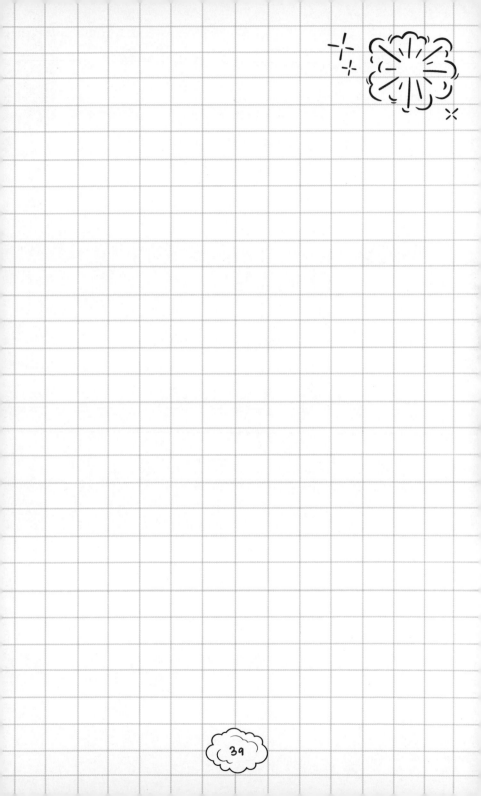

One unique way to be awesome is to create a secret identity. In addition to being a great friend, Dee Dee doubles as Samantha Jade, Private Eye, an expert in spying, climbing with a grappling hook, acting, and many other talents. Check out her full list of skills here.

SKILLS

Roller Skating	Debunking
Frizbee	Flamenco-Standing
Extreme Frizbee	Wu-Tanging Jazz
Cycling	Jazz Dance
Recycling	Jazz Flute
Card-Counting	Jazz Wands
Ice-Sculpting	Jazzercise
Tomfoolery	Jazz-Fu
Confrontation	Over-Acting
Ghost-hunting	Miming
Under Acting	Scene Stealing
Rapping	Mountain-Climbing

What are some special skills or exotic talents that you want to develop?

Oh, no! Chad looked away for just a second and all of his friends disappeared. Solve the maze below to help Chad find Nate, Teddy, Francis, and Dee Dee.

START

FINISH

It's another *Samantha Jade, Private Eye* mystery! Help ~~Dee Dee~~ Samantha Jade spot six things that don't belong in the shot below:

I've gotten into some pretty close scrapes here at P.S. 38. Luckily, my friends were always there to bail me out. Write about a time when your friends had your back.

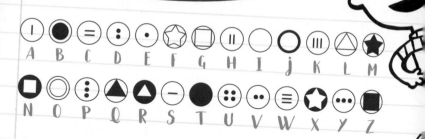

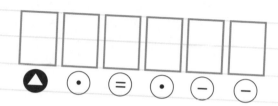

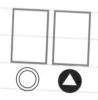

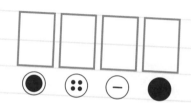

I have pulled off some pretty impressive pranks in the past, leaving me pretty pleased with myself. Write about a time that you were proud of yourself. Was it a solo accomplishment or something you worked on with others?

Take a good long look outside the closest window. What do you see? Blue skies? Maybe trees? Whatever it is, it's way better than being stuck in detention! Mrs. Godfrey is video calling her cats; now's your chance to get away! Solve the maze below and enjoy your afternoon!

START

FINISH

Zeff may be the hardest-working guy in town! He's popping up everywhere, from the pizza shop to the pest control van, to the pages of this very book! Connect the dots and color him in when you're done!

ZEFF

Mrs. Godfrey. Around here, we call her the *Creature Teacher*, and I'm sure you can see why! Spot four differences between these two pictures before she can fill out a detention slip!

Ahhh, the playground at P.S. 38. Or is it? Use **Nate-O-Vision** to turn this place into something special!

How many words can you make out of the name
CHAD APPLEWHITE?

CHAD APPLEWHITE

_____   _____

_____   _____

_____   _____

_____   _____

_____   _____

_____

I gotta say, math and social studies just aren't my thing! Use this page to write about a time that you were bored. What did you do to break through the boredom?

Our class lizard, Sheila, has gone missing and they're saying it's my fault! They're right, but they don't have to say it. Only one of these routes will lead Sheila back home safely, so make sure you pick the right one!

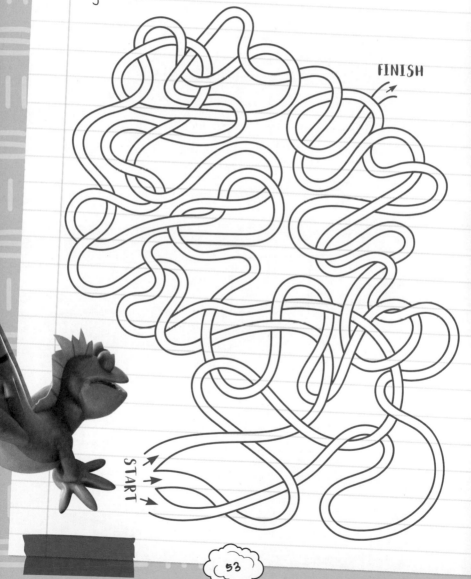

FINISH

START

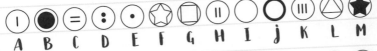

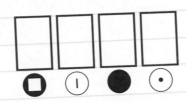

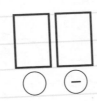

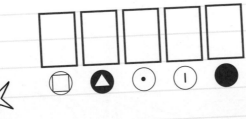

I always say that "being awesome is ninety percent attitude and ten percent imagination." Okay, well I don't *always* say it, but I'm workshopping it. In the meantime, use that ten percent to create a new comic!

Sure, I'm a role model here at P.S. 38, but I'm not the only expert on being awesome. Check out this Q&A with *Big Nate* creator, author, and cartoonist Lincoln Peirce and check out the activities on the pages!

Where do you get your ideas?

When I started the comic strip, a lot of my ideas came from my own memories of middle school and the kinds of events or situations most people experience during those years: school dances, pop quizzes, gym class, and so on. But over time the characters have grown and changed, and I've also also introduced a lot of new characters. And as a result, I think most of my ideas nowadays are driven by the characters' personalities: Nate is filled with misplaced confidence, Chad is sweet and innocent, Dee Dee is a drama queen, etc. The richer the characters are and the better I understand their strengths and weaknesses, the easier it is to think up scenarios that highlight their personalities in funny ways.

56

How long does it take you to draw a comic strip?

The actual drawing of a daily strip doesn't take very long at all— somewhere between one and two hours. A Sunday page is bigger, so the drawings take longer. But that's only half of the process. The more important half, which is coming up with a good idea in the first place, can make producing a finished strip more time-consuming than you might think.

I could probably make the drawing part go faster if I used a digital tablet, like a lot of my cartoonist friends do. They can correct their mistakes or redraw something in no time at all on an iPad or a Cintiq. But I'm not a tech-savvy person; I can't imagine myself switching over to digital at this stage. Plus, I genuinely enjoy making a strip the old-fashioned way. I like drawing with pens on paper, hand-lettering all the dialogue, and so on.

Try creating your own funny comic strip!

What comics did you enjoy growing up? Are there any cartoonists who were an infuence on your work?

I always cite Charles Schulz's *Peanuts* as my number one influence, and I'm definitely not alone in that department. Virtually every cartoonist I've ever met grew up as a *Peanuts* fan. But there were tons of other strips I loved as a kid: *Andy Capp*, *B.C.*, *Tumbleweeds*, *Fred Bassett*. When I got a bit older, *Doonesbury* by Garry Trudeau became hugely important to me. And in high school—keep in mind this was the pre-internet era before you could find anything online—I discovered some old collections of comics from the Golden Age: strips like *Krazy Kat*, *Thimble Theatre*, *Polly and Her Pals*, *Terry and the Pirates*, and many others. I'm not sure how much they influenced my work, but they were certainly inspiring. And a little intimidating, too, because the artwork in those strips is incredible.

What are your favorite comics and graphic novels?

1.

2.

3.

4.

5.

6.

7.

8.

9.

10.

What do you do if you get writer's block?

I'll usually just take a break from working and do something else for a while, like go for a bike ride. A little break in your routine can often spark some fresh ideas. It doesn't always work, though. Sometimes you just have to think your way out of it.

You can use this space to brainstorm some ideas for your next comics creation! Who would the characters be? What kind of adventures will you have?

61

Do you have any pets?

I grew up with a Cairn terrier named Rufus, and our kids grew up with a wonderful mutt named Scout. I'm sure I'll have another dog someday, but I haven't decided yet what kind to get.

What are your top 3 names (each) for a dog, a cat, a hamster?

DOG NAMES:

1.

2.

3.

CAT NAMES:

1.

2.

3.

HAMSTER NAMES:

1.

2.

3.

62

Who is your favorite Big Nate character?

This might be a boring answer, but Nate is my favorite character to write for. It's easy to brainstorm ideas for him because he's such a bundle of contradictions. On the one hand, he's a can-do person who's obsessed with himself, which means he's always coming up with ridiculous plans to get famous or make money or set a world record. On the other hand, he also spends a lot of time complaining about things or people he doesn't like, which makes conflict a constant part of his life. And confict is an engine for driving interesting stories. People wouldn't read *Big Nate* if Nate got along well with all his teachers, or if he accepted every situation without making a fuss.

Who is your favorite character in the *Big Nate* universe and why?

How did you turn the comic strip into a TV series?

I've done a little bit of everything. When the TV show was in development, I created a "bible" in which I wrote very detailed descriptions of each and every character in the strip—everyone from Nate to School Picture Guy to Sherman the classroom gerbil. Later on, I consulted on the character designs and did a bunch of drawings for the animators to use as guidelines for certain facial expressions, body language, and so on. But I'm most involved with the writing. Like all TV series, *Big Nate* has a team of writers, and together they turn ideas into outlines and outlines into scripts. They send the first draft of each episode script to me, and I do "punch-ups." That might mean trying to make a joke funnier, or it might mean rewriting a character's line so that it sounds more authentically like the way that character speaks in the comic strip. Sometimes if I think a scene is confusing, I'll send notes to the writers asking them to clarify exactly how or why something is happening. I do a lot of rewriting. Sometimes the writers will use about half of my suggestions, and other times they use almost all of them. As long as I feel I've made each episode just a little bit better, I'm happy.

What was the coolest thing about seeing your comic strip turned into an animated TV series? Did anything surprise you?

I was definitely surprised, in the happiest way possible, by how great the characters look in the show. Having drawn the strip in two dimensions for over 30 years, I was a little skeptical about how the characters would look in 3-D. I was particularly worried about Nate's hair, because it's so unusual and such an essential part of his physical appearance. But the designers at Nickelodeon are the gold standard, and they did a tremendous job on all of the characters. And the coolest part? It was when I saw Nate move on screen for the first time. The art director and I had spoken at length about some types of animation we both really liked, and one of the examples was the stop-motion "puppet" animation that you see in Rankin-Bass Christmas specials like Rudolph the Red-Nosed Reindeer or The Year Without a Santa Claus. The way the characters move in Big Nate is smoother than that, but it still has a modified herky-jerky quality that's reminiscent of stop-action. At a certain point in the development process, Nickelodeon showed me a 4-second clip of Nate jumping up onto a desk, teetering on the edge, and falling off. It was great. I think the animation in our show is second to none.

What advice do you have for people who also want to be cartoonists, writers, or animators?

I don't think it is enough to have a story to tell; almost everyone has stories in their head that they find interesting. The key is finding a way to tell a story so that OTHER people find it interesting, too. You learn how to do that by practicing your craft. For cartoonists, that means working to improve your writing, first and foremost. Being able to draw is wonderful, but writing is the foundation that everything else is built on. A comic strip with great writing and mediocre art is much better than a comic strip with great art and lousy writing. My other piece of advice is: You learn what makes a good story by reading a lot of good stories. I think it is important for aspiring storytellers to read all sorts of writing: fiction, non-fiction, newspapers, magazines, blogs, comics, graphic novels. Read 'em all!

If you decided to write a book or a comic series, what kind of interesting stories would you tell? _____
_____
_____
_____
_____

Would you write them as a written story, a graphic novel, or as a script for a movie or TV show? _____
_____
_____
_____
_____

Who would be the audience for your story? What do you think they would like about it?
_____
_____
_____
_____
_____
_____

Teddy is one of my best friends and the perfect partner in crime. Except he always disappears when we get caught! If he thinks he's pulling a fast one on me today, he's got another think coming! Spot five differences in the images below before Teddy vanishes!

~~Dee Dee~~ Samantha Jade swears she's getting into the rhythm of this gumshoe gig! Help her find six things that don't belong in the scene below.

My friend Dee Dee is the best actress I know!
There's nothing she loves more than getting into
character and putting on a show. If you could
take one event from your life and turn it into a
play, what would it be?

Help Dee Dee find everything she needs before her big show tonight!

```
Z j C O M E D Y S W L B D B A
E W Q E E V H L j Y C X B N C
N I G W U R N A L I N E S Y T
U T M A S K E M U S I C A L O
Y C N S K C R H C D P j O N R
C F D X N O H A E I I H R T W
S C K F L S Y A D A R E Y F X
T S U P R T S P R M R E N A D
A C A B T U C S A A N S W C A
G L U H V M R H M D C K A C E
E X K R W E I O A Y X T W L G
W Z Q F T C P W H D Z F E X W
C W P H L A T M B F O Q j R L
O W X D P W I R Y E R O V S H
E K W F H B C N K T Z I E K D
```

REHEARSAL   COSTUME   STAGE   MASK   SHOW
CHARACTER   CURTAIN   ACTOR   SCRIPT
AUDIENCE   MUSICAL   COMEDY   DRAMA   LINES

DOODLE PAGE

Ugh. My dad said if I'm making an activity book, I have to include the family. How many words can you make out of the name ~~Dad~~ **MARTIN WRIGHT?**

MARTIN WRIGHT

_____ _____

_____ _____

_____ _____

_____

_____

_____

_____

Do you have siblings? My sister, Ellen, is super NOT awesome. What do your siblings do that annoys you? What do you (holds nose) love about them?

My art teacher, Mr. Rosa, is always saying that I "need to find a creative way to channel my self expressions." Not exactly sure what that means, but I'm always down to doodle!

A normal hallway at P.S. 38, right? Not if you have **Nate-O-Vision!**

Dogs are the best! I really want one, but my dad says I have to practice by walking Spitsy instead. What other kinds of pets can you have?

```
I Q K J O R K Y N D O D
T I B B A R E V D B O R
C A T K O M Z T T Z S G
D G N O C Q K D S H O T
W F A T R S D R M M U P
I I F M J M K I H R A W
G S N W F O U B T C Z H
U H Z L H J I L U D L N
O G U J M G E B N Y Y Q
Y G U I D J U V I R S V
O W Y A S I V Z Y K I C
U N G M B B W Y X E W Q
```

RABBIT CAT DOG BIRD
HAMSTER TURTLE FISH

Jenny Jenkins? The love of my life! How did she get in here? You know what? There's a lesson here about playing it cool. Take a deep breath and find four differences in the pictures below.

Kim Cressley. Yes, I've heard the rumors and we are *JUST PROJECT PARTNERS.*

Out of boredom, I made an embarrassing list of things I love about school! Help me find it and cross off anything on the list!

```
Q D P I F K P N G R W Z W E R
M D A I C C Q A E E F F M V E
Z O C J H V C B E X O I O H C
V A G R O C F K G S T V L F E
C L T G X M E J E H S B Z N S
N W Q B Z N J E C V H E C B S
S Y H G D W D N W T B C C P M
T U Q S O Z U R E C E S S E M
A A M I L L X L Y F K Y Y Y R
Q T H M W O U T S I N Y I D S
V M D U E V H V O Z V N E L S
L K A S Y R Z K F D D N O K Z
K K F C S T F Q L K B E K X S
C F R A Y N N L P Y Y J F L D
L L A B R E H T E T C B K D K
```

JENNY   RECESS   TETHERBALL
LUNCHTIME   RECESS   WEEKENDS
RECESS
SUMMER

I ESPECIALLY LIKE RECESS

How many words can you make from the name
Dee Dee Holloway?

DEE DEE HOLLOWAY

Francis is always getting straight As. Help him find what he needs to study!

```
C T G R H W T T S X N C T K G
V O E L E E O F A T O N I J K
P C M X D R A R D S Z R R N G
X P D P T Y A D K A R V T O V
Q E W U U B K S P S T N K T K
G N V P G T O Y E H H P X E Q
E C H Z Z Q E O U R O E W S U
V I W B V W I R K Q A N E Y I
P L D Q Z N W H K S P G E T E
Q S C A L C U L A T O R S S T
```

HEADPHONES
COMPUTER
PENCILS
CALCULATOR
WORKSHEET
NOTES
TEXTBOOKS
ERASER
QUIET

83

People say that I'm a bit of a troublemaker, but I prefer to think of myself as an "excitement-maker". Write or draw in the thought bubbles to see what I'm thinking!

NOW THAT YOU'VE HAD SOME PRACTICE DECODING, THIS SECRET MESSAGE SHOULD BE A BREEZE!

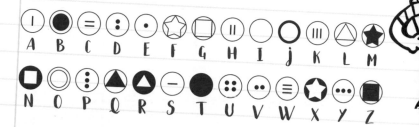

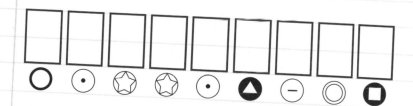

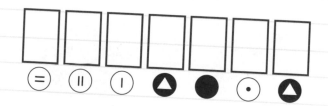

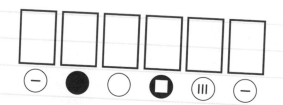

I may have pulled off my greatest prank yet! Of course, Principal Nichols disagrees. *HELP?!*

START

FINISH

You can't spell Nate without skate! Okay, you can, but they still rhyme. Help me find the quickest way home by untangling these lines!

FINISH

START

Bored before class? Challenge a friend to a game of tic-tac-toe! The first person to connect three of their symbols wins!

If you can believe your eyes, you've stumbled into another *Samantha Jade, Private Eye* mystery! Help her solve a mystery once again. The game is *a foot*, or something! Can you spot four things that seem out of place.

DOODLE PAGE

Rocking with my band is where I'm king!
If you had a band,

Who would be in it? _____

_____

_____

What kind of music would you make? _____

_____

_____

What would your band be called? _____

_____

_____

What would you call your fans? _____

_____

_____

What instrument, if any, would you play? _____

_____

_____

Help Fear the Mollusk get ready for our next show by matching the characters to their instruments!

Francis has been called our friend group's "Voice of reason," but in this exercise we're looking instead of listening. While he details his latest worries or fun facts, find four differences between the two photos.

Principal Nichols is responsible for the day-to-day running of P.S. 38 and making sure the school has enough money to keep the lights on. One time he even hired a crew of monkeys to help fix up the school. Big mistake! What crazy scheme do you think is on his mind now?

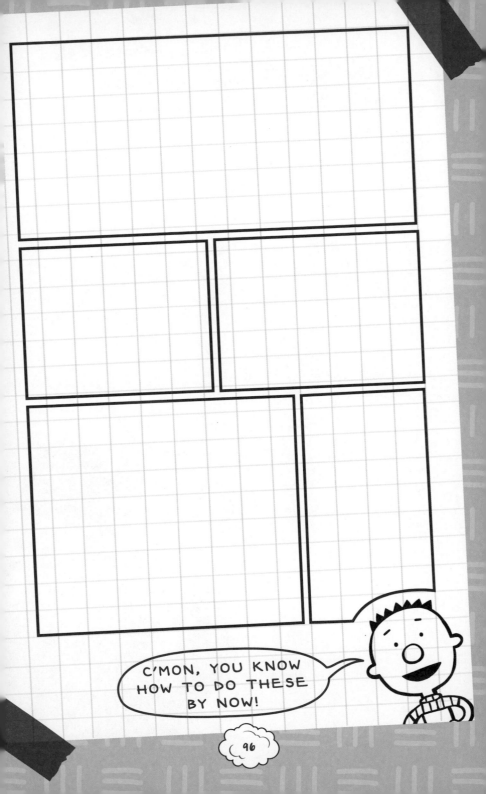

You still with us? Learn an important lesson in **The Art of Cool** by crossing out my name whenever you see it below and putting the remaining letters in order.

NATENATENATENATENATENATEINATENATE
TNATEANATENATENATENATEINATENATEN
NATETNATEENATENATENATEANATENATES
NATEYNATENATENATEBNATEENATENATEI
NATENATENATENATENNATENATENATEG
NATENATENATEANATENATENATE
NATENATENATENATENATENATENATE
NATENATEWNATENATENATENATEE
NATENATENATENATENATENATESNATE
NATENATENATENATEONATENATEM
NATENATENATENATENATEENATE

____ ____ ____ ____

____ ____ ____ ____ ____

____ ____ ____ ____

It's school picture day, the most nerve-racking day of the year. Help everyone look their best for the yearbook by coloring in their Picture Day outfits! Draw your own yearbook photo, too!

DRAW A PORTRAIT OF YOURSELF HERE!

98

Everyone's pictures turned out so well! But what if they hadn't? Grab a pen, pencil, or marker and doodle over everyone's yearbook portraits. Eyepatches, mustaches . . . you know what to do!

Francis says he's been "tutoring" at Jefferson Middle
School, but I think we all know what that means . . .
They're holding him hostage for his big juicy brain!
Solve the maze below to help us get Francis back
from Jefferson!

START

What's happening at my house? Use **Nate-o-Vision** to decide!

What do fire-breathing dragons dream of? Hoarded gold? Old caves? Fill in the bubble over Mrs. Godfrey's head to see what's on her mind.

DOODLE PAGE

I don't want to speak too soon, but I feel like you're getting the hang of this. Create your own connect the dots here and challenge a friend to complete it! Bonus points* if you draw extra details like a face on a person, or windows on a house!

* A reminder, bonus points may not be exchanged for dollar bills or ice cream.

Ellen? Come on, why are we even giving her space? Fine, fine. Find four differences between these two pictures, then turn the page as _fast_ as you can.

Part of the fun of art is developing your own style!
Use the blank grids below to re-create the looks of
Teddy and Dee Dee!

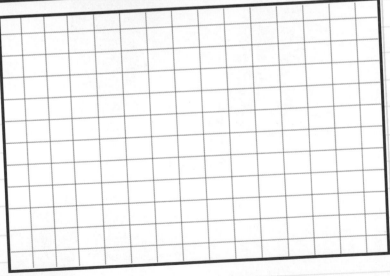

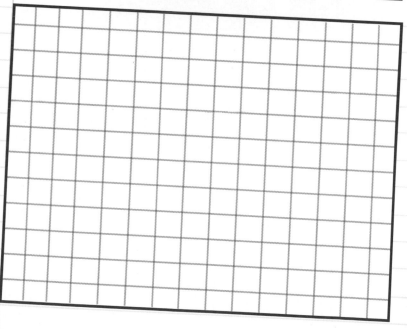

As you could see in my ~~personal disaster area~~ locker earlier, I'm known for my fondness for snacks. Use **Nate-O-Vision** to draw some of my (and your!) favorite foods around the breakfast table.

How many words can you make from the name
Jenny Jenkins?

JENNY JENKINS

_____   _____

_____   _____

_____   _____

_____   _____

_____   _____

_____   _____

_____

I can see our activity book is coming to an end, so . . .
let's make one more comic together. For old time's sake.

It's Zeff's first day with the company van! What company? I'm not even sure he knows at this point, but do him a solid and solve the maze to help him navigate his deliveries!

START

FINISH

ANSWER KEY!

PAGE 7

PAGE 11

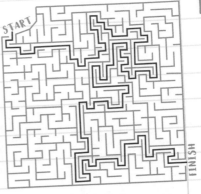

PAGE 14

PAGE 17

PAGE 19

PAGE 20
START

PAGE 25
COOLEST
KID IN
SCHOOL

PAGE 30
START
FINISH

117

PAGE 31

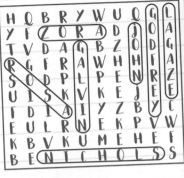

PAGE 32

PAGE 34

PAGE 37

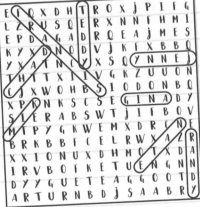

PAGE 42

START

FINISH

PAGE 43

PAGE 45

R E C E S S

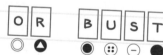

O R   B U S T

PAGE 49

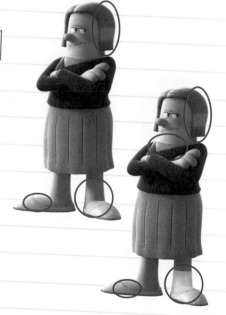

PAGE 47

START

FINISH

PAGE 53

FINISH

START

PAGE 54

N A T E
○ ① ● ⊙

I S
○ ⊖

G R E A T
▢ ▲ ⊙ ① ●

PAGE 69

PAGE 68

PAGE 71

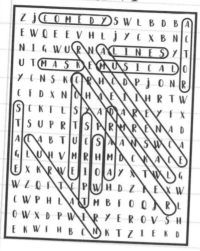

PAGE 78

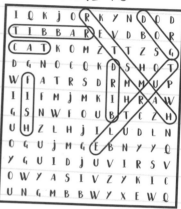

PAGE 79

PAGE 80

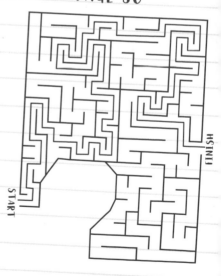

START

FINISH

PAGE 81

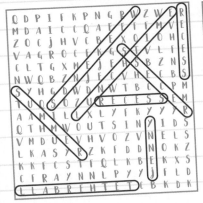

PAGE 83

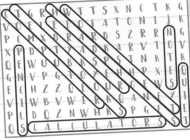

PAGE 85

PAGE 86

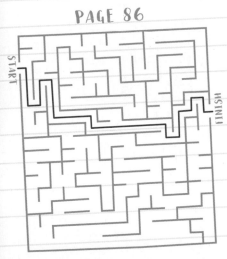

PAGE 87

PAGE 89

PAGE 93

PAGE 94

PAGE 97

I T   A I N T

E A S Y   B E I N G

A W E S O M E

PAGE 102

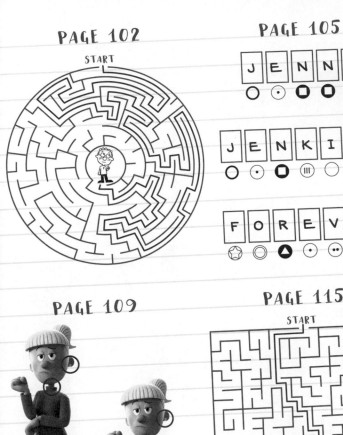

START

PAGE 105

J E N N Y
○ ⊙ ▢ ▢ ⋯

J E N K I N S
○ ⊙ ▣ ⦀ ○ ▢ —

F O R E V E R
✩ ◎ ▲ ⊙ •• ⊙ ▲

PAGE 109

PAGE 115

START

FINISH

Well, that about does it! If you've taken these lessons to heart, you should be well on your way to being almost as awesome as I am! If not, then I'm sorry to say that you're a lost cause and you need to give this book to someone it can help. Until next time . . .

stay awesome!

Andrews McMeel Publishing
a division of Andrews McMeel Universal
1130 Walnut Street, Kansas City, Missouri 64106
www.andrewsmcmeel.com

Author: Terrance Crawford
Designer: Jessica Meltzer Rodriguez

Special thanks to Jeff Whitman, Nathan Schram, Jarrin Jacobs at Nickelodeon,
and to Lincoln Peirce for editorial guidance throughout this project.

23 24 25 26 27 RLP 10 9 8 7 6 5 4 3 2 1
ISBN: 978-1-5248-8223-5

Made by:
Shenzhen Reliance Printing Co., Ltd.
Address and place of manufacturer:
25 Longshan Industrial Zone, Nanling,
Longgang District, Shenzhen, China, 518114
1st Printing – 4/3/23

ATTENTION: SCHOOLS AND BUSINESSES
Andrews McMeel books are available at quantity discounts with
bulk purchase or educational, business, or sales promotional use.
For information, please e-mail the Andrews McMeel Publishing
Special Sales Department: sales@amuniversal.com.

Complete Your *Big Nate* Collection

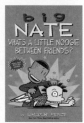

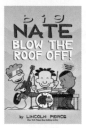
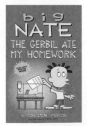